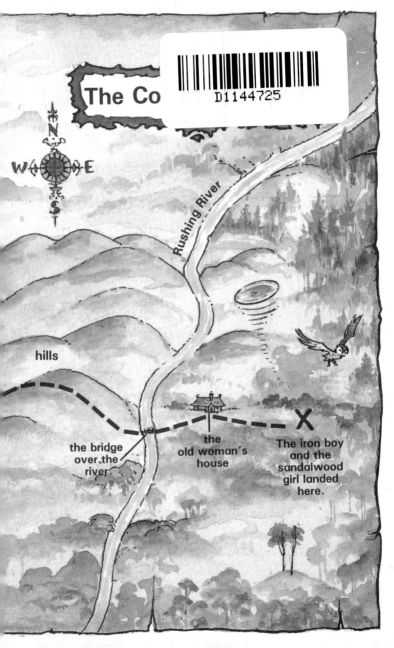

USING THIS BOOK

One of the best ways of helping children to read, is by reading stories to them and with them.

If you have been reading earlier books in this series, you will be used to reading the story from the left-hand pages only, with words and sentences under the illustrations for the children to read.

*In this book, **the story is printed on both the left and right-hand pages**.*

*The first time you read the book, read the **whole** story, **both** left and right-hand pages, aloud to the child and look at the illustrations together.*

When the book is next read, you read the text on the left-hand page and the child, in turn, reads the text on the right-hand page, and so on, through the book.

British Library Cataloguing in Publication Data
McCullagh, Sheila K.
    Fire in the grass. —(Puddle Lane. Stage 4; v. 4)
    I. Title   II. Davis, Jon   III. Series
    428.6   PE1119
    ISBN 0-7214-0969-5

First edition

Published by Ladybird Books Ltd Loughborough Leicestershire UK
Ladybird Books Inc Lewiston Maine 04240 USA

Fire
in the grass

written by SHEILA McCULLAGH
illustrated by JON DAVIS

This book belongs to:

_____

Ladybird Books

A boy made of iron and
a girl made of sandalwood
had come to the magical
Country of Zorn.
They wanted to grow up,
and to be really alive.
The Magician had told them that
they must go to the Blue Mountains,
and bathe in the Silver River.
Then they would become
like other children.

The iron boy and
the sandalwood girl,
stood on the hill
in the Country of Zorn.
As the sun came up behind them,
they saw the Blue Mountains.

The mountains were a long way away,
and their tops were covered in snow.
The iron boy and the sandalwood girl
saw a wide valley in front of them.
It was very hot.
"Look – there's a river in the valley,"
said the sandalwood girl.
"We can follow this path to the river."

The iron boy and
the sandalwood girl
set off down the path
to the river.

The sides of the valley
were covered with dry grass.
The grass shone like gold
in the sunshine.
They had not gone far,
when they saw a hare.
The hare was sitting
at the side of the path.
The hare was startled.
"Who are you?" she asked
in a frightened voice.

"An iron boy, and a girl
made of sandalwood,"
said the iron boy.
"We are going to the Blue Mountains,
to look for the Silver River.
Don't be afraid.
We won't hurt you."

"You are going on a
dangerous journey,"
said the hare. "Don't you know
that fire dragons live in the valley?
They can breathe fire.
If they see you, they will
set the grass on fire, to stop you
going to the Blue Mountains."

"I'm not afraid of fire,"
said the iron boy.
"I'm made of iron.
Iron doesn't burn."

10

"But I'm made of wood,"
said the sandalwood girl.
"I'm afraid of fire."

"We must find another path,"
said the iron boy.

11

But as they turned to go back,
they saw smoke behind them.
"It's too late," cried the hare.
"The fire dragons have set fire
to the grass! Quick!
Run down to the river,
and hide under the water!"
The hare turned, and raced off
down the path towards the river.
The iron boy heard
the crackle of fire, and the grass
behind them burst into flames.

"Run!" cried the iron boy.
The iron boy and
the sandalwood girl ran
down the path towards the river.

At first the grass was nearly
as tall as they were.
But as they ran on,
they came to a place
where the grass had been cut.
The stalks were only
as high as their knees.
They could see the river
in front of them, not far away.
But the crackle of the flames
behind them was coming nearer
and nearer.
Suddenly, a big red dragon
stepped out on the path.

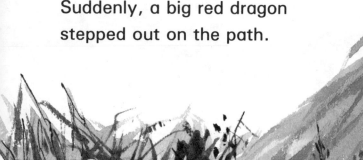

A flame shot out
of the dragon's mouth.

The grass in front of them
burst into flames.
As quick as a flash,
the iron boy picked up
the sandalwood girl.
(She was very light.)
He held her high up
above his head.

He ran past the fire dragon,
and down the path
to the river.

The iron boy reached the river.
It was wide and shallow,
and full of rocks.
He set the sandalwood girl
down in the water, and together
they made their way to some big rocks
in the middle of the river.
"Are your feet burnt?"
cried the sandalwood girl.

"No," said the iron boy.
"I'm made of iron.
I could feel the flames,
but they haven't burnt me."

The iron boy and the sandalwood girl
sat down in the water,
by the rocks.

The grass flamed along the bank,
and for a few minutes
it looked like a wall of fire.
Then the flames died away,
and nothing was left
but blackened grass, and smoke
drifting up into the blue sky.
''You were just in time,''
said a soft voice.
They looked up, and saw the hare.

The hare was sitting
on one of the rocks
in the middle of the river.

"We still have another field of grass
to go through,
before we reach the trees,"
said the iron boy.
"Are there fire dragons
on the other side of the river?"

"Yes, there are," said the hare.
"You mustn't go that way.
Cross the river and then follow it,
till you come to a cave in a cliff.
The silver ponies fly down at night
to eat the silver moss
that grows in the cave.
The silver ponies will take you
to the Blue Mountains."

"Thank you, Hare. You have saved
our lives!" cried the sandalwood girl.

The hare didn't stay to listen.
She went on, across the river
jumping from rock to rock.

The iron boy and the sandalwood girl
followed the hare,
but they went very slowly.
The sandalwood girl was so light,
that she would have been
carried away in the rush of water,
if she hadn't held on
to the iron boy.
When at last they came to
the other bank, the hare had gone.
There were no fire dragons,
but they didn't go into the grass.

They set off along
the bank of the river.

The sun was just beginning to set,
when at last they turned a corner
and saw a grey cliff ahead.
There was a big cave in the cliff.
It was growing dark, but the cave
shone with a faint silver light.

As they came to the mouth
of the cave,
they saw silver moss
growing on the walls.
The moss shone like silver fire.

"This must be the cave
the hare told us about,"
said the sandalwood girl.
"Let's wait here, and see
if the silver ponies come.
I'm very tired."
They sat down in the mouth
of the cave, and waited.

The sun set, and
the moon came up.
It shone down into the cave.

The sandalwood girl was so tired,
that she had gone to sleep,
when the iron boy suddenly
gripped her arm, and whispered,
"Look!"

Three silver ponies were flying
high over the river.
The moonlight shone on their wings.

As the sandalwood girl and
the iron boy watched,
the ponies swung around,
and flew down into the mouth
of the cave.

The sandalwood girl stood up.
''Ponies, silver ponies,''
she said softly.

The ponies were startled at first,
but the sandalwood girl
spoke so softly, that
they stayed to listen.
''Ponies, silver ponies,''
said the sandalwood girl.
''We have to go to the Blue Mountains.
We have to bathe in the Silver River,
so that we can become truly alive.
Will you take us there?''
The ponies breathed softly.

"We will take you there,"
said one of the ponies.
"We will take you
to the Blue Mountains."

"We cannot take you
to the Silver River,"
said another pony.
"The banks are too steep.
But we will take you to a place
where you can see the river,
as it plunges down the cliff.
We have come here
for the silver moss.
Wait while we eat, and
when we have finished
we shall fly back to
the Blue Mountains.
We will take you with us."

So the iron boy and
the sandalwood girl waited,
and the ponies ate the silver moss
that grew in the cave.

When the moon began to set,
the ponies were ready.
They moved out of the cave.
One of them knelt down
on the bank of the river,
and the sandalwood girl
and the iron boy
climbed up onto his back.

The pony ran along the bank,
and opened his wings.

The iron boy and the sandalwood girl
felt the pony lift under them.
The ground dropped away,
and they flew up into the sky.

They flew over the grass.
They flew over the trees
in the forests below them.

They flew on and on,
over the hills —

— until at last
they came to the Blue Mountains.

Notes for the parent/teacher

In the stories in the books at Stage 4, the child is asked to read part of the main story and not just the sentences under illustrations. This is a big step forward.

If you read the whole of the story to the child first, it will make the reading much easier for him or her. But some children still need the chance to read quietly to themselves the pages that they will later read aloud with you.

Reading a story aloud on sight, without having had a chance to look at the text first, is one of the most advanced and difficult kinds of reading. If, when the child is reading aloud, he/she reads the words in such a way that the story makes sense but the words are not exactly the same as those in the book, don't correct this on a first reading. This shows that the child understands the meaning even though he/she gives that meaning in his/her own words. On later readings, you should ask the child to look carefully at what was there in the book. The illustrations will give lots of helpful clues.

Remember always that both you and your child should **enjoy** your reading sessions. Keep the book, even when the child can read his/her part of it easily and has gone on to other, more difficult books. Children will later reach a stage when they can read the whole story for themselves.